Still

Look

the Same

FARZANA DOCTOR

YOU

STILL

LOOK

THE SAME

© FARZANA DOCTOR 2022

All rights reserved. No part of this publication may be reproduced, stored in a retrieval system, or transmitted in any form or by any means, graphic, electronic, or mechanical — including photocopying, recording, taping, or through the use of information storage and retrieval systems — without prior written permission of the publisher or, in the case of photocopying or other reprographic copying, a licence from the Canadian Copyright Licensing Agency (Access Copyright), One Yonge Street, Suite 800, Toronto, Ontario, Canada, M5E 1E5.

Freehand Books acknowledges the financial support for its publishing program provided by the Canada Council for the Arts and the Alberta Media Fund, and by the Government of Canada through the Canada Book Fund.

Freehand Books
515 – 815 1st Street SW   Calgary, Alberta   T2P 1N3
www.freehand-books.com

Book orders: UTP Distribution
5201 Dufferin Street   Toronto, Ontario   M3H 5T8
Telephone: 1-800-565-9523   Fax: 1-800-221-9985
utpbooks@utpress.utoronto.ca   utpdistribution.com

Library and Archives Canada Cataloguing in Publication
Title: You still look the same : poems / Farzana Doctor.
Names: Doctor, Farzana, author.
Identifiers: Canadiana (print) 20210379472
Canadiana (ebook) 20210379480
ISBN 9781990601057 (softcover)
ISBN 9781990601064 (EPUB)
ISBN 9781990601071 (PDF)
Classification: LCC PS8607.O35 Y68 2022 | DDC C811/.6—dc23

Edited by Sharanpal Ruprai
Book design by Natalie Olsen
Printed on FSC® certified paper and bound in Canada by Marquis

For my mother, Banu
my father, Shamoon
my sister, Fariya
—my first true loves.

CONTENTS

I

Blame it on childhood 1   3

Lost in the breakup   5

Solitudes   6

Just fine   9

Judging other people's breakups 1   11

Revisit   12

Couples therapy   13

Blame it on childhood 2   14

In transit   16

S.T.U.G. reactions   17

Judging other people's breakups 2   18

Stretch marks   20

Fall back   22

II

How to get wifi at Jamia Millia in 14 easy steps   27

Ziyarat   29

After Rumi's "Who Makes These Changes"   31

Red Fort   32

The twins of Bogotá   34

Swipe left   35

Blame it on childhood 3   37

It didn't happen with the others   39

LEIRVIK   40

Hot yoga   43

Carried away   44

Tarot goodbye   46

Forty-three   48

III

Boundaries 53

Some days are like that 54

Dear Jibon 55

Open mic at Beirut Helem 57

Universal apathy 59

Date night 61

How love is 63

Perimenopause 65

Rockette lines on Queen West 66

New Toronto 69

A Khatna Suite 70

IV

The beauty of us 83

Nikah mu'tah 85

Three years in 88

You still look the same 91

Learning Lebanese 93

Brothers and sisters 95

Ageing 98

Sky in my veins 99

Attached 100

Find me 101

Never alone 103

I

THERAPY HOMEWORK

describe your world ending
in as few words as possible.

One day we left home,
forgot to lock the front door,
terrible mistake.

Blame it on childhood 1

I learned how to fish on YouTube
she shrugged,
yup, bait and lures
lines and knots,
now I teach angling!

Together we list
every skill learned
through screens,
stuff our parents
didn't teach us.

Bake carrot cake.
Propagate lilies.
Win Scrabble with 'xylem.'
Hold a tree pose.

Balance a budget.
Divide assets.
Refill a fire extinguisher.
Defrost the freezer.
Assemble a bed.

Ask someone out.
Identify an attachment style.
Spot a narcissist.
Break up over text.
Fix a scratch on a car.

Fade stretch marks.
Manage hot flashes.
Dress your age.

Lose weight.
Fake body positivity.

Hack an ancestry website.
Relearn, then forget
a mother tongue.
Dialogue with your inner child.

Apologize meaningfully.
Stop apologizing.
Perform salat.
Write a haiku.
Say I love you.

Lost in the breakup

One blue pillowcase,
part of a set.
I've searched
every musty closet.

Where are all the good knives?
I guess they were yours.
Sorry I took them
for granted.

That old bike pump, gone.
It was five—no six—
months of hard pedaling
before I bought a new one.

A loaf pan, probably mine?
After a dozen years there's no way to know
but chalo,
I've stopped baking.

Potholders gifted to us,
charred from being left
on a crimson burner
the day you moved out.

The entire top floor
of our house, disappeared.
I still hear your footsteps
overhead.

Solitudes

I

Across common wall,
Tim's pleas
like toes testing
an eroding cliff.
It was a mistake!

Emily's accusation a siren:
You cheated on me!
Footfalls, slamming door.

I murmured a prayer
for the nice couple
who'd moved in that spring:
> *May they not know this grief.*

Two nights later
watering faded lilies,
I toss over backyard fence:
How's Emily?
> *She moved out.*
Before I could console,
he was gone.

Three overcast months
CBC wafted through plaster
The Current and *Q*
broadcasted twice daily
radio voices where hers used to be.

II

Frigid morning
I awake to wailing,
pull duvet to ears.
Neela, upstairs tenant
bawls and paces,
crazing a new worry line
in my ceiling.

Two had come to view the place,
one moved in,
the breakup
a day after lease-signing.
We crossed out her name,
initialled change.

My shy text stumbles upstairs:
You okay?
Her reply tumbles down:
Sorry if I disturbed you.
I long to write:
> *I know this grief.*

III

And I wonder:
have my neighbours heard
the new solitude
whispering within these rooms?

As I ash my bedtime cigarette,
do they see me
inhaling the night?

When I unlock the front door
do they watch me
from their porches?

Just fine

The key worked,
not sticky like
you'd worried.

Our dog sprung
past me,
a search for you.

She skittered upstairs,
I followed, not wanting
her to get into things
she shouldn't.

The old feather duvet
fits your new bed.
Maggie leaped up,
rumpled sheets,
it wasn't me.

A race downstairs,
whine at side door.

Apricot blush along fence,
Asiatic lilies dug from my yard,
divided, transplanted,
thriving in your garden.

Your wraparound porch,
just-purchased patio chairs
—red and white striped
like circus tents—
cheery. Perfect
for summer Scrabble games.

Funny, how easy
I insert rosehip tea
citronella candle,
hand in velveteen bag,
wooden tiles,
your winning word.

And so I cry
in your kitchen
shiny toaster my mirror
while our dog watches,
ears drooped low.

I won't tell you
any of this,
perhaps not for years,
instead send a text
*the key worked
        just fine.*

Judging other people's breakups 1

(for E & D)

He wanted to bring a bouquet
like he did the last four times
you launched a book,
knows you adore lilies.

But he's no longer the one
seated beside you,
clasping your damp hand
your beaded clutch on his lap.

Now, at back of room,
he claps, laughs,
heartburn rising, maybe
he shouldn't have come.

He's bought this new novel,
dedicated to your fresh love,
isn't sure whether to queue
for an inscription.

In his dim bedroom,
he'll read your lines
twice over,
hoping to find himself
inside them.

Revisit

I put daal out to thaw,
but the old yogurt container
from back of freezer
was your soup.

Bubbling in pot,
scotch bonnets
fired up air.

After so long
surely it had turned?
Spoon to mouth,
a peppery taste.

Then another and another
and another.
Bowl emptied, stomach full,
mind wandering,
heart wanting.

Three hours later,
cramps and tears.

I clear out the freezer,
chip away
two years of ice.

Couples therapy

We hadn't a clue
what to do—
it was like half the roof caved in,
frayed electrical wires
sparking slow
smoulder through plaster.

What if help had arrived
in nick of time,
a magic brigade
with those long hoses,
ladders that reached second story
—and blankets, we'd need those too—
rescuing us
from our burnt out home?

And later, fresh air
balm and bandages for burns,
a season of recovery.

Would it have made any difference?

Blame it on childhood 2

Minutes after the news
of her death
your father hugs you
        we have to move on
which for him means
departing at dawn
returning after sunset
daily marathons
to outrun grief
        try to keep up

but fathers can feel lonely
you notice his cracking voice
when he remembers
his disappeared wife
urges you to visit her grave
doesn't want to go alone

a housekeeper hired
then a second
a third
each tormented by daughters
who can't bear a woman
not their mother

one stays a year, June
her name a death month
but also springtime
blue-eyed cockney exotic
daily oven-fresh pastry
comfort temporary
as a contract

at school
you're still the Indian girl
now more strange
friends play freeze tag
join them
play hopscotch
play kissing tag
only adults ask questions
when you stop
to catch breath
rub skinned knees
     (Aren't you sad?
     Didn't your mother just die?)
keep playing
     try to keep up

your sister, sweet fifteen
finds a stoner boyfriend
with a licence and beater
to pick her up
take her away

quit Girl Guides
quit Judo
quit friends
no one to drive you

solace in Duran Duran
daily double episodes
Young and the Restless
20 Minute Workout
Family Feud
     try to keep up

In transit

hugs at Departures
security pat downs
hidden nail clippers

ten-minute manicures
chair massages
shoe shines

waxed floors
wheelie bags
moving sidewalks
whizzing carts

auto-flush toilets
sunglass kiosks
low-interest credit cards

five-dollar water
bulk candy
multi-faith prayers

panicking latecomers
last-minute gate changes
staticky announcements

inert carousels
lost luggage
expectant faces at Arrivals
getting my own Uber home

S.T.U.G. reactions

S.T.U.G.: Sudden
Temporary
Upsurge of Grief,
a term coined by
Dr. Therese Rando.

This morning the sky, blue.
If clouds were moving in
I didn't notice.

Winds whipped up,
I called it a breeze,
believed my Gujarati shawl
was protection enough.

And then slow drizzle
became sleet,
frigid wind turned
hair to ice.

Uphill into the gale,
blizzard obscured vision,
I crashed into a snowdrift.

Judging other people's breakups 2

(for FS and her seniors' trailer park friends)

You couldn't meet Ellie's eyes,
instead shaded yours,
focused on chapped lips.
Happened at the Esso down the road.

> Ellie and Stan
> next-door winter Texans,
> seemed a happy couple,
> invited the entire park community
> for their golden anniversary.

She stuffed crimson impatiens into clay pots,
punched down loose soil.
Forty-four done—
a memorial,
a gaping mouth—
around the side of their trailer.

Six un-potted plants
wilted in midday heat.

*We stopped in for a fill,
he said, 'Ell, you know how I hate goodbyes.'
Then he walked past the pumps,
got into some brunette's blue Mazda.*

> You'd already heard
> that gas station detail at bingo,
> whispers between B-10 and I-18.

Just as you were about to ask,
she muttered, probably

the umpteenth time,
I have no idea who that woman was.

You cooed sympathy,
weedy pep talk:
better off now,
no guarantees,
live each day to the fullest.

     Really, your mind travelled
     north to the husband who'd left you
     for that student with the glittery lip gloss,
     exceptional thesis.
     You'd bought an Airstream Bambi
     drove south each October
     pretended widowhood
     in the Lone Star State.

You watered her dry plants,
and just for a moment,
petals flushed,
dusty leaves green again.

I wake up each morning,
the taste of gasoline
on my tongue.

You set down watering can,
held empty pots for her,
dry clay scratching hands
while she shoved in the last
of the desolate plants.
You both needed gloves,
carried on anyway.

Stretch marks

Why am I so scared? Miriam asks.
I didn't use to be like this, Tami says.
I nod, solemn
as we three stand in a row
atop Jumping Off Rock,
awaiting courage.

One by one
we move to cliff's edge,
look down, say:
Yes, now.
1 . . .   2 . . .   3 . . .

toes inch back.

This middle age,
skins marked
by births and ink,
sagging tits.
I wonder why stretch marks
don't make a body more supple.

Tami leaps,
a mid-air gasp,
    splash.
Miriam, with mock scream-face
steps forward
            and I,
not wanting to be left behind,
close eyes,
plummet.

Icy water
jumper cable shock
awakens flesh,
I'm fifteen again
diving under
somersaulting,
surfacing,
with a stupid wide grin
for a great big world.

I shake off
to the rhythm
of internal '80s soundtrack
—*name myself Rio*
and dance upon the sand—
scale rough rock
barely notice
scratched palms,
pink welts rising on thighs
from the rush
back up.

At the top
a pause.

Why does the cliff seem
higher now? Tami laughs.
And I think:
yes, we didn't use to be like this.

Fall back

Daylight savings, you say:
let's see 2 am twice,
shut down the club
you and me
and all of humanity
sweating gratitude
onto beer-drenched floors.

My head aches,
limbs leaden—
can't I just have
an extra hour of sleep?

With wide eyes
goading grin
you ask: but what if
this hour   is a silver locket
holding every shiny wish?

I close my eyes, think:
            any wish?
I'd sit hip-to-hip
with mom on a park bench
show her all my Girl Guide badges,
read my valedictorian speech,
offer a tour of my garden.

I'd ask her if it's true
she visits me in dreams
flickers overhead lamps
leaves me coins, feathers,
played matchmaker
so I'd trust love again.

I'd beg a slide show,
her thirty-eight years alive,
eleven when she was mine,
colour in outlines
memories long faded.

I'd press her
for stories
her final forty minutes
the forty days after
and the forty years since.

I'd use every expansive second
seek her advice,
capture every detail,
hold her hand,
for by the end of the hour
she'd be gone.

| |

THERAPY HOMEWORK

describe the process
of middle-age self-searching
in as few words as possible.

*One airline ticket,
two years of online dating,
but what did you find?*

How to get wifi at Jamia Millia in 14 easy steps

1. Go to the first office where a man with a handlebar moustache will direct you to a second with a green tie and the correct application form.

2. Affix a current passport photo, write your father's name on line four, remember your temporary cell number.

3. Cross muddy campus field, admire water lilies in garden pond, smile at young women reading Premchand in weak Delhi sunshine.

4. Drink chai with the department head whose thick hair reminds you of a Bollywood star, his name, tip of tongue, eluding you.

5. Carry his signature to the second office, supplicate to Green Tie who will shake his head, point to the next desk over.

6. Hold your tongue when a man with a shiny pate says a three-line paragraph, not previously requested, is now required.

7. Speed dial the department head, seek administrative rescue.

8. Prepare yourself when Bald-ev remains resolute, and even Department Head Shah Rukh Khan (yes! That's it!) is not exempt to procedure and must phone Department Head #2 to plead your case.

9. Department Head #2 will greet you with a slight bow, pressed palms, tranced-out smile and will sing-song the necessity of this-and-that policy. Sigh into his calm face, nod, gather your things.

10. When you stand he'll insist that *you* mustn't traverse this sodden campus. Rather, like the Queen, he'll press a red button, summon a thinner, older, browner man.

11. *He* will jog on your behalf, deliver wilting page to Department Head Shah Rukh Khan, while Department Head Deepak Chopra pontificates on immigration trends that made you a stranger to his country.

12. When Jogger-Uncle returns with the completed document don't high-five him. Instead, smile, red-faced, while Deepak ushers you out of his office, back to where you started—two hours, one cup of chai, five desks, many men ago.

13. Although no less indifferent, Moustache Guy will tap permission into his keyboard.

14. Exhale and try not to grumble like a foreigner.

Ziyarat

Ziyarat: a visit to a holy place

I slip on Maasi's rida,
drape myself in modesty,
in disguise
as a good Bohra girl.

Our suicidal rickshaw
snakes through Bombay streets,
a pilgrimage
to Raudat Tahera.

Raudat Tahera:
mausoleum for the
leader, or Syedna,
of the Dawoodi
Bohras (an insular
Shia subsect).

We slip off shoes,
pass through gate,
the bearded attendant nods,
as though I belong there.

Inside, cool and hush,
rubies spell Allah on marble walls,
a golden casket
tomb's centrepiece.

Like a tourist, I watch
women circling,
pushing in line
to kiss a coffin.

We join the queue,
I study acolytes' faces,
search familiar features,
intrude upon averted eyes.

My turn, I hurry,
mimic supplication,
can't remember the dead man's name
even though I've asked twice.

A woman approaches,
Maasi makes introductions,
the sister nods,
as though I belong there.

You look so much like her.
I am recognized
as my mother's daughter
motherless daughter.

Immobile, a shard of religion
hits me,
penetrating through shroud
reaching for my chest,
and in crypt's half light
my mother is with me again,
clutching my damp hand,
her rida brushing mine.

The moment, quicksilver,
I reach for my Nikon,
am told I can't, although
souvenirs may be purchased outside.

In sunshine,
I reclaim shoes
don't buy a postcard.

Maasi snaps my picture instead,
a promise to remember the day
my mother hovered over me
in disguise
as a good Bohra girl.

After Rumi's "Who Makes These Changes"

Who makes these changes?
I speak a thousand words.
The wrong one echoes.
I run after affection and find myself
chased by a ghost.
I invite everybody
no one RSVPs.
I cook lavish meals for dozens
and eat alone.

I should be suspicious
of what I want.

Red Fort

(for Vivek)

Red Fort: a historic
site in Delhi that was
once a residence of
Mughal Emperors.

Half hour queue,
stray glances at souvenir stalls,
no, trinkets can wait.

Finally, she scans my purse,
he punches my ticket.

I rush through the palace
linger at metal barriers,
pulled to prohibited
interior chambers.

Maybe it's imagined nostalgia,
diasporic sentimentality.

An invisible force
grabs my wrist,
prods with sharp fingers,
whispers in a tongue
I once knew:
you're back
after so many years.

Pants, shirt, shoes
stripped away,
I'm wrapped
in threadbare sari,
pushed into familiar courtyard,
rough stone
scrapes feet.

Is that you standing there?
Even with your back turned
I recognize the shadow.

Glance over shoulder,
your steady gaze meets mine.

I blink
    alone again
    among sightseer crowd,
    catch breath,
    spin around
    search for you.

    Later I'll tell you
    of traversing time,
    insist I once
    lived in the Red Fort.

My words will sound
wrong, foolish:
I was once a servant there,
one of many
with no claim to those walls
yet it was home
for three decades.

Rascal smile
spreads your face wide
but I believe it when you say—
you feel the same way
about the Red Fort, only,
you were once its queen.

The twins of Bogotá

Late for work
I read the entire essay:
two sets of identical twins
switched at birth
mixed and matched
into fraternal pairs.

Journalists, CNN voyeurs,
psychologists watched the four men
make sense of mistaken
belonging and me too,
I clicked, baited,
coffee burning in my pot
while I consumed
the real-life telenovela,
just one of eight million
liking the article—
maybe all of us
imagining a reunion
with our reflections,
and just for a second
a fragment of unbelonging
    falling away.

Swipe left

The research question: what's it like to be a straight girl
looking for love?

My design may be flawed, but after many dates,
countless online interactions to understand your customs,
I've reached an interim hypothesis:

your men
are a problem.

Perhaps that's not accurate;
I have no control group and my subjectivity
is the consistent dependent variable.

My data suggests direct communication
is not a norm. There is much *baby, baby, smile for me*
and jokes that go one beat too far.

I don't profess expertise in linguistics.

A colleague suggests my sample is skewed,
that there are precisely twenty-one straight cis dudes
ruining dating apps for everyone.

I don't disagree with that theory but doubt its accuracy.

It's easy to recruit subjects:
an ounce of ethanol, a single survey question,
they'll follow you home.

I stand by my method of observer immersion.

An interesting finding:
they think they are taking you to bed
even when it's your key turning the lock.

My funding allows me to employ my dog,
secondary researcher to assess subjects at door.
I document carefully the length and quality
of each sniffing episode
and whether she rolls her eyes or sits for a treat.

A confounding variable:
once, and only once did she snarl
(at a tall white man who wore a fedora and smelled of
    desperation).

I dropped him from my study.

Quixotic reliability? Each and every time
I introduce queer theory into the interview
the subjects reveal one identical porn fantasy.

The most significant part of the experiment
is not the most pleasurable
and vice versa.

I'm not always certain how to code pillow talk—
qualitative data tumbles from lips
leaves stains on my pillowcases,
outlines lingering for weeks—
I've recorded thirty-one percent tenderness
combined with sixty-six percent white supremacy
and seventy-two percent mansplaining.

At the end of the project
I will deactivate my account,
ghost my participants,
won't present any findings.

Blame it on childhood 3

Dad's Volvo,
mustard, the safest colour
he'd boast,
heavy metal shell,
armour that won't crumple
even in the worst collision
hardest impact.

His fender-benders,
sideswipes,
a T-bone,
never seemed to leave
a single bruise.

You bought your own
yellow Volvo
but every time you drive
new dents form,
old scratches deepen,
rust criss-crosses paint.

Best to put the clunker in park,
wrap it in a tarp,
prop it on cinderblocks,
let the grass grow tall underneath.

But you can't help
turn the key,
rev the engine
just to hear it roar.

Careful at first,
you stay out of traffic,
grow bored after eleven miles,
veer off country roads into rush hour,
tail-gate,
honk rage,
careen through red lights,
drive the wrong way
on one-way streets.

It didn't happen with the others

No, with pointed ringed fingers
I found everything wrong
untidy, inconvenient.

But with you, when thorny burdock
pushed through floor's cracks
I mistook them for purple lilies.

When grey mice
raced through the living room
how did I confuse them
for turquoise-winged birds-of-paradise
beautiful and rare?

LEIRVIK

The porn amateurs
digitally fumble,
performing
a threesome
on my screen.

An elbow bumps a thigh,
a knee jerks,
hits a chin,
she says *aaah!*
He says *ohhh!*

I can't decipher
what the other gal feels,
her body mimes
something like ecstasy.

Camera shifts,
scans footboard.
Hey! Their bed!
It's just like mine.

I compare our Ikea frames,
faux iron flourishes,
ninety-nine ninety-nine on sale,
a bitch to assemble
with those tiny Allen keys.

The triad finishes
apparently satisfied.
I lean against
identical headboard
click Replay.

This time
the first woman winks at me,
the guy beckons.
Hand to my chest
I whisper: *me?*

The second woman
raises her eyebrows
as though to say
Her? I didn't agree
to a foursome.

Awkward, I press Pause,
plump up pillows, tap Play.

Gal No. 2 says:
It sags
What?
The mattress, dummy.

The other two ignore us
kissing and rubbing,
writhing and moaning
but she comes in for a close-up.
It's cheap, she says.

Looks good at first
but the paint will peel.
I wish I'd sprung
for a BRIMNES
with generous storage
for bedtime reading.

I get what you mean,
I reply, wide eyed,

this one, so princessy
but MALM has underside drawers—
way more practical.

Live and learn.
I nod at her sage advice,
we say goodnight.
I bookmark her
so we might meet again.

Hot yoga

During the first downward dog
between my legs,
I spied a ponytail
swinging
like a pendulum.

We turned toward the mirror,
I stared into our reflections,
but her focus, a single point
over my head.

Her tree stood tall,
mine swayed.

Next, wide-legged forward bend,
cobra, sphinx.
Inshallah she didn't see
I can barely touch my toes.

Then we did
pavana mukta asana,
also known as
wind-releasing pose.
Someone near me farted,
I hoped she didn't think
it was me.

During savasana
sweat stinging eyes,
I inhaled humid air
imagining it was her breath,
mentally rehearsing
how I might say
namaste.

Carried away

Your text tone
a gentle wind chime,
chosen special,
it doesn't suit you at all.

I react near-Pavlovian
to mechanical tinkling,
delude myself thinking
it's a trick I taught myself.

I glance at the screen,
tempted, look away,
don't want to be in the breeze
of your words, not today.

I return to the moment,
my footfalls on country road,
wild lilies growing in ditch,
fallow fields.

Across a wire fence
a lonely horse glances,
won't come closer
although I beckon.

You text again,
bells clamorous,
clang-clanging
in hot wind.

I palm my phone,
inhale, read,
unsure what else to say,
I reply, *okay*.

Heart pounds dissent.
When I look up,
the sky darkens,
rain threatens.

Pocket the phone,
say goodbye to the horse,
who, smarter than I,
trots to shelter.

Quicken my pace,
down the road
the church's spire
shudders in the gale.

Another gust shakes your chimes,
thunder rolls somewhere far off
rain pours down,
soaking me.

Again your summons
I lose my balance,
upended, pulled into
your funnel cloud.

I rise over the church,
spin past the horse's pasture
knocked unconscious,
the tornado carries me
to you.

Tarot goodbye

She squints over my cards,
Seven of Cups,
Three of Swords,
indicators you and I
have crossed paths before.

Husband in one life,
lover in another.
Did we switch genders
last time?—
she thinks you were once
my unhappy wife.

For two goddamned centuries
it's been the same old argument:
> *Why won't you change?*
> *Why won't you?*

When I turn over the Tower card
lightning flashes across starry sky.
Ten of Swords stabs my back.

It's hard for me to say,
but I will:
go away.
Battle our long lingering
urge to stay.

In this life and the next
may we circle one another
only in dreams,
from across continents,
perhaps, allowing
separation of seas.

May we fill other cups,
pull the Lovers card anew,
our fates finally turning,
may you not turn up
in my poems anymore,
the cycle forever ending.

Forty-three

By the age of forty
you're supposed to have stopped caring
what people think—
that's what *Vogue* says.

Late bloomer, I guess,
at forty-two I step into my wardrobe,
inhale dust motes, switch on light
avoid full-length mirror.

Toss every wire hanger
to floor, separate
garments too snug
for a Ladies Size Twelve body.
One bag garbage,
one bag charity,
nothing sparks joy.

.On weighted down ten-speed
pedal hard to Lansdowne Value Village
drop my load,
linger long at automatic doors
leaking musty air.

I wish transformation were so easy—
who doesn't want to keep
that polka-dotted halter top
from when you were nine,
the striped skirt Auntie
said was slimming?

I dart inside,
purchase a beret too tight
for an adult head,
yank it over unruly hair.

I wear it for three days,
Hat whispers: *shrink some more.*

I go Vegan-Keto-Paleo,
do the 7 Minute Workout forty-two times,
squeeze myself into exercise bras
short-shorts,
one-size-too-small pumps.

My head aches,
blisters bubble at heels,
waistband digs a trench around belly.
New date says: *you look sexy.*
I blush and swoon.

I grow bored with cottage cheese.
One day, naked under hot shower
I expand, rebound,
flop onto double bed,
starfish,
take all the space.
My date topples off,
bewildered, stomps feet, yells: *Crazy! Irrational woman!*
Door slams
and I nap.

The tiny hat takes flight,
as do the tight shoes, little shorts,
giving chase, mewling: *please don't go.*

When I finally awake,
I am forty-three.
All that remains:
a pair of scuffed sneakers,
forgotten size-twelve dress.
I don this armour, step outside.

III

THERAPY HOMEWORK

describe trauma and its sequelae
in as few words as possible.

*Ask me in two days
if I am really okay.
Delayed reaction.*

Boundaries

yours are tensor bandages
stretchy yet firm
holding you in
keeping tendons warm
injuries protected

mine are band-aids
from back of drawer
never the right size
adhesive dried up
they slip off
at awkward moments

I wish sometimes
especially when
—or perhaps before—
I skinned a knee
sprained an ankle
I had your first-aid kit

Some days are like that

Count the seconds
between one breath,
labour through the next.

Count the minutes
to salute the sun
just once.

Count the hours
until it's dark enough
to shut eyes.

Count the weeks
waiting for snow
to stop falling.

But then, an interruption
a pause at 11, 28, 43
lose count.

Ticking halts,
feet touch cold floor.

Maybe, go to window,
notice allure of grey clouds.

When street lamps alight
watch flurries dance in the glow.

Without checking the clock
know it's past midnight,
you can rest.

Dear Jibon

A week after Christchurch
minutes past Fajr
message via Facebook
a single word: hide.

First assumption:
you are among the legions,
lonely Muslim men saying hi,
spellcheck hyperactive.

But no, your profile pic,
young brown man
hanged, lynched, dead.
I squint, zoom in.

Who is he?
What happened to him?
Heart pounds, reflex,
lock the door.

Your name, Jibon Joti,
click, scan
a nothing profile,
vacant identity.

Google says maybe
you misspelled, stolen
from a Bengali soap opera
I've never watched.

Second assumption:
you are among the legions,
lonely white men saying hi,
white supremacy hyperactive.

I picture you
searching for Muslims
people who look like me
sending a single word
to thousands,
your hope to instil fear
in the wake of Christchurch
in the wake of Ardern,
biker gang solidarity,
new gun laws.

Just to be safe,
confide in others, check
double check:
            should I be afraid?

Dear Jibon Joti:
hide your nothing,
hide your vacant,
I know who you are.

Open mic at Beirut Helem

Tonight's event, a contest.
C'mon up!
Yalla yalla!
Tell us your best lie.

The first three spin
silly tales,
easy laughter.
I squirm in my seat,
look to my friends—
how long can it stay funny
at Beirut Helem?

Everywhere, closets
are mazes. Lost,
you turn back only to find
someone's locked you in,
whispering God's name,
guarding the key.

But Alhamdulillah
the stories tonight
are about exits,
some as small
as cat doors.

Next up a young man
grabs mic in both hands:
I went to nursing school
plausible nightshifts,
pious excuses
to dance cheek to cheek
with my boyfriend.

Then a woman in ripped jeans:
Can you believe?
I make up imaginary friends
Leila, Noor, Yasmine!
When my parents ask I don't
reveal Habiba, Rony, Haneen.

Stories echo through the hall,
my heart an anchor
solid, sinking.
I remember, whisper
Bismillah-ir-Rahman-ir-Rahim.

The winner,
last to take the stage,
a wistful hijabi:
My mother suspected,
but begged me
to spare her
the truth.

Universal apathy

(for Fatme)

Learning Arabic,
I get stuck at ayn
frustrated by a consonant
that looks like a number,
sounds like a vowel.

I fear I'll never get it right.
Wikitravel's colonial explanation:
To say this letter, use the throat muscles
just like when
> *you are throwing up.*

I practice with an everyday phrase:
Chou badna n3amell?   Whatcha gonna do?
I cough it out
to evoke sympathy, be funny
show off, fit in
but it's during Trump's first February
I finally comprehend
its mix of universal apathy
and Lebanese zen.

I hear its echo everywhere,
words fluttering up from a million windpipes,
white seagulls circling Lebanon's turbulent seas.

Later, with Fatme,
we discuss laws that allow rapists
to marry victims instead of jail
and before I can stop them,
the words are up my esophagus,

spewing from mouth,
so well-travelled they no longer
require effort:
Chou badna n3amell?

Her eyes spark anger,
mouth wide open,
tongue depressed,
uvula exposed
to emit a thundercloud:
Laizem n3amell shi!   We must do something!

My throat dry, empty.
Laizem n3amell shi?
How have I never heard
this expression before?
Laizem n3amell shi.
Why did I not seek
this translation?

I store this phrase in my gullet,
ready myself for spring.

Date night

You text: *I'm here, love.*
I grab keys, purse,
rush outside
blink at your face
through cracked windshield.

What a thrill!
This new relationship
energy of teens
pulses through
middle-aged veins.

I unlatch car's door,
you reach for me
too quick too hard,
    I am a twitchy animal
a rescue,
afraid of hands.

I shrink,
mild fawn smile
careful
to not upset.

You lean back
ask what's wrong,
a part of me
could tell you
but I don't:
        I've gone away
      I've gone away.

I don't know
why it happens.

I might despair
    I wanted you tonight
only you,
not this fright.

Or perhaps I'll turn
away, simmer
at what you did
or didn't do
    wrong, point blame
for this madness.

You interlace
our fingers
a gentle lead,
I could resist
but I don't.

I allow your tug
meet your gaze
remember your name
exhale the fear
come back.

I know why
this happens.

How love is

Nightie bunched around thighs
monster at foot of bed.
It's there, it's there!
I yell into
thick mist.

Your voice night-ragged
It's okay baby,
just a dream.

Don't believe you
heart attack
going crazy
already dead
save me.

Clumsy grab pulls
my face to warm chest,
too close, too tight,
but I can breathe,
open my eyes,
your embrace
not a cage.

In the morning
we will share dreams,
Remember?
That intense one last night?

You'll frown,
rub eyes
I don't recall.

But you held me,
until I was no longer afraid.
You'll shake your head
my nightmare
eluding you.

Sometimes I wonder
if this is how love is for you,
something you do
in your sleep.

Perimenopause

Mid-morning,
dense fog descends,
visibility low, nothing
flying out of here today.
Best to shut down,
face grey sky
wait for gloom to clear.

> What to do about
> loss of words,
> arguments I can't win,
> this interminable grounding?

One a.m.
I am a red ember,
my rage glowing
in the dark
long after everyone
has turned off lamps.

> The world tossing,
> turning me,
> sun-deprived skin slick
> with mad sweat,
> body simmering
> in forty-odd years
> of bullshit.

Rockette lines on Queen West

June third we drive
through sunshine,
traffic lazy.

Middle of street
a man backs up
shoulder checks
aims phone at a daisy chain,
young women
posing, skirts long
golden hair loose
blowing in the breeze,
smiles, easy.

We wait
as he photographs
the birthday party,
bridal shower,
synchronized swim team.

Light turns red,
ample time to gaze
upon sidewalk group.
I exhale
my inevitable query:

Where are all your
racialized friends?

I close window,
the question
doesn't escape,
hums in tune
with car's engine.

We carry on
through Queen West
past Trinity Bellwoods'
white circles,
gatherings of happy people
sunning themselves,
then up to Dundas
to eavesdrop on
white conversations,
none of them about
the missing ones.

The question louder now,
a droning beehive
as we move through
this stolen city
where we are no longer
your visible minority
and yet
you look no different.

Yes, of course,
every so often,
an exception
a disruption
to the Rockette lines.

But what I really
want to know:
in the Instagram records
of fun-filled Saturdays,
brunches and galas,
board meetings,
writers' unions,
clothing swaps

neighbourhood potlucks
why am   I
still your
visible minority?

The question's noise
builds, deafening, undeniable.
We must
pull over, park.

New Toronto

On my way
to end of street
lakeside meditation rock
a red-winged blackbird
raging, nest-protecting
dive-bombs, clawfoot
digging into scalp
tipping me
forward.

Our echoing shrieks:
go away
go away.

I flee
to steadiness
of boulder
splash of lake
duck glides past
consoles
Your initiation
to the neighbourhood
complete.

I rub my head
at the bluntness of birds,
tread more carefully
on the way home.

A Khatna Suite

Khatna is a form of female genital cutting practiced by Bohras. It is considered to be a religious requirement by the Syedna (religious leader) and is thought to make seven-year-old girls naik (sexually pious). It is conducted by both amateur cutters and medical doctors. Elder female relatives enforce the practice.

1. Zainab

Sometimes I can forget
what you did
in the name of
    Allah
        Syedna
            community.

But there are nights
alone in bed
when all I feel is
your stamp of shame
    my body numb
        my mind
            too awake.

You told me I'd be
a true Bohra woman
but it's during
these moments
    I am sure
        I am no one
            to you.

2. Rumana

Detroit born and raised,
went to medical school,
earned my parents' praise.

Graduation, nikah,
baby boy, baby girl,
duplex near jamaat.

> We are good Dawoodi Bohras.
> We are good people.

My mom came to me
when my niece turned seven,
said it was my duty.

> When I was young,
> we went to Gujarat.
> I can still picture
> that old lady's dirty flat.

> I bled quite a lot.
> Sometimes
> (it's probably
> all in my mind but)
> I can still feel it down there.

> We are good Dawoodi Bohras.
> We are good people.

Word spread quickly—
they came to my house
two or three monthly.

I moved to a clinic
the procedure more
professional, quick,
sterile, with good lighting,
I hand out lollipops
so it's less frightening.

We are good Dawoodi Bohras.
We are good people.

3. Twitter Trolls, aka, Bohra Women for "Religious Freedom"

You're lying!
It's just a tiny nick.
It's my religious right.
It makes our girls clean.
It's the same as ear piercing.
It doesn't cause any real harm.
You are inventing your trauma.
You feminists just want to get famous.
Do not tell me what is best for my child!
You are making our community look bad.
Because our Syedna, in all his wisdom, says so.
You're not really Bohra. So you can't speak for us.
It's been happening for centuries—why protest it now?
It's all about equality. What we do to boys we do to girls.
Yes, it does enhance the woman's pleasure in her marriage.
Shame on you! Why must you speak about such personal things?
You should be protesting what happens in Africa, not this small ritual.
We're an educated community. Why would you think we'd harm our children?
It's not really female genital mutilation. Stop making a mountain out of a molehill.

4. Grandmothers

In your granddaughter's whispers
    maybe in her dreams
to social workers
in courtrooms
inshallah
    in verse
you will be named.

You will be named
for glorifying bearded men
who never recognized your glory
for not questioning
for not knowing the questions.

I get it, you wanted her
to be naik
because you felt dirty.
For inheriting violence
passing it down—
I'm sorry but
you will be named.

Even if she doesn't recall
the afternoon of promised candy
her body will remember,
you will be named.

You'll never go back
to when she buried her face
in your lap, rida and belly fat
her pillow.
No.

After, didn't she
flinch at your touch?
This is naming too.

Do not fool yourself.
She may never speak
a bad word, may
defend you
to your blessed grave
but you will be named.

You will be named
        by me
by she
by us.
We will speak
into silence
until there is
a cacophony of voices
shouting Syedna's name.

5. An imagined mithi sitabi for seven-year-olds

Mithi sitabi: a special-occasion meal, normally held for women's milestones. It starts with a prayer and continues with a ten-course meal of traditional savory and sweet foods eaten in a thaal.

I

Gather the youngsters
not just girls
but boys too
and the kids
who teach us
the breadth and splendour
of gender.

First, the lesson!
Spin a globe
remind them who they are:
children of Gujarat
before that, Yemen
today, settlers on other lands.

Share stories of Allah,
make eyes glow
harvest moons
on clearest nights.
Invite them to believe
        or not.

There will be no talk
about allegiances to rogues
who make empty
        promises.

Instead, speak of ties
to cousins
great-great grandmothers
smog-damaged trees
elephants and bumblebees.

Suggest they close eyes
sense whispers from within,
pulses beneath skin.

Instruct them to serve
kindness, to prepare
extra plates for unexpected guests.

Make them remember
we are a learned people.
Urge them to read Lorde and Rumi
turn ears to Ila Arun and iskwē
paint fingernails and landscapes
voice a hundred impossible-
to-answer questions.

Confess our blunders
how we spurned siblings
defaced our women
set ablaze neighbours' homes
accepted false gods
worshipped gold
believed
we were the chosen ones.

Ask them
to be better
    to be gracious
        to be merciful.

II

Next the jaman!
Seat them seven to a thaal
pour water from silver chalamchi lotas
over small outstretched hands.

The first course
a pinch of salt
obeisance to hadith that insisted
white crystals would save us
from seventy diseases—
leprosy, madness
ourselves.
Tell the children
we now understand
this was a lie
fabricated by men
God knows why.

Bring the rest of the food
all a nod to the sweetness of life:
tablespoon of kulfi
sliver of cake
circle of jalebi
jube jube
cube of burfi
slice of mango
pista mithai
gummy bear
and finally another pinch of salt
to test the tongue.

A second hand washing,
distribute certificates—
proof of attendance—
coloured outside-the-lines,
decorated with stickers, felt
and glitter.

IV

THERAPY HOMEWORK

describe healing and recovery
in as few words as possible.

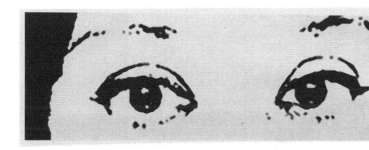

**Then, out of the blue
you followed me on Twitter,
I no longer cared.**

The beauty of us

You're a chocolate face,
sun-burnt Melissa Miller's
Grade One insult.
　　So what. You're a vanilla face,
my mother's coached words
did not help.

Small town Whitby:
Tuesday afternoon Brownies,
daily Lord's Prayers,
Friday evening Gujarati classes.

　　Paki go home,
fourth-grader Michael Bolton,
armpit-stink blur,
shook salt over my scalp
white crystals sharp,
wounding,
I scratched all day.

My mother dissolved
violence under shower's spray,
no more tears shampoo,
telephoned Ed Broadbent,
booked an appointment
to end the cruelty
of school children.
　　And we are not even from Pakistan!

I refused to go.
　　She went without me.

Years after the cancer took over,
years after I tried to forget her,
years after I shunned the pre-meds who looked like me,
years after I streaked my hair blond,
I remembered her fury,
        stepped into its petticoat,
wrapped six yards of livid silk
around child-bearing hips,
draped pallu across heavy breasts.

Before the mirror,
I admire her brown face,
adorn our hair
with fragrant white lilies,
see the beauty of us.

Nikah mu'tah

I was hoping for a sitcom mosque
like the one on the prairie
          (wrong geography, but)
with the handsome imam,
inside jokes, camaraderie.
Instead, in St John's, Newfoundland
it's an industrial building
overlooking a salami factory.

We've come here
this auspicious day,
our six-month anniversary,
invited our parents
          (just the dead ones)
witnesses for the ceremony.

At the metal door, we're blocked.
          Sister, you go up to the gallery.
We dawdle
          (unaccustomed to separation)
your first time in a Canadian mosque
and I'm unsure what to do
about segregation.

I submit,
climb stairs.
You pass
through men's doors.

Nikah Mu'tah: a
temporary and
privately performed
marriage, with
mutually pre-agreed
(time-length and
behaviour) terms,
practiced by some
Shia Muslims.

From behind glass
I try to spot you,
back away
when the one who called me Sister
        (eyes on my chest)
stares up.
I find my modest place
against the wall,
hurry through prayers,
descend, find you outside.

We improvise,
hide behind minaret
        (self-conscious—can anyone see?)
search the internet
find correct oaths
mouth words
that join you to me,
unceremoniously.
In the car I complain
too rushed, not special,
you shake your head
        what did you expect?

At Signal Hill, I insist
a re-do, looking eastward
across vast ocean,
I slip leather bracelet over your wrist
declare myself temporarily married
for a period of six months,
to be renewed
if we wish.

Hours later,
you gift me my mahr
        (as specified, twenty-dollar earrings),
eat ice-cream sundaes at a Chinese restaurant
and you ask again,
this time, gently:
        no really, what did you expect?

I want
a place to belong
where someone like you
someone like me
are blessed by Allah and community.

I want to marry
myself to you
for the defined period
for the agreed-upon dowry
in a place of
half-truth,
half-fiction.

Three years in

Back when segmented sleep was common, this period
between "first" and "second" sleep inspired reverence.
— JESSE BARON, *New York Times*

I convince you to accompany me,
a month of dorveille,
ignore electricity,
succumb to sunset,
wake at one am,
for two quiet hours.

In the seventeenth century
they'd tend wood stoves,
read by candlelight,
ponder visions just dreamt.

Not insomnia—
that modern fretfulness—
but a starry sky rousing,
obedience to ancient
bodies' rhythms.

I have set an alarm
but that's not cheating,
nor is a clip-on book light.
I am ready, journal and novel
stacked beside me.

You stir, push pillow over head,
I remind you
of our *New York Times* experiment:
C'mon, let's try something new?

You shuffle off to pee,
I start a poem
first stanza flowing
divine, sort of.
You return with your laptop,
I scold: *No Netflix.*

I leave you to your Koran,
pleased with 1:15 am
spiritual undertakings,
close my eyes in meditation,
twitch awake to WhatsApp chime.
You're texting?

I shake my head,
crack spine
of the Booker-winning novel
I've been meaning to read.

Five pages in
the scent
of my distraction
reaches you
and we pause
our deep thoughts,
stroke a thigh,
hold a hand.

Are we allowed to do this?
you ask, all snark,
I report:
lovemaking was normal at two am.

I'm reminded
of when we first met,
time irrelevant,
night blended to morning,
sleep inconsequential,
love   easy,
like a breeze through
a half-open window,
or like falling,
limbs slack,
breath deepening,
drifting off,
into an altered state.

Next morning
blinding sunshine,
screech of alarm,
we hit snooze.

You still look the same

(for Suzy)

We met in Grade Two,
had Mean Miss Edmonds.
This is my memory not yours.

I learned the term
Best Friend that year,
claimed you.

Together, we went to Brownies,
swam with Dad,
weeded Mom's lilies.

At recess
a boy called you Paki.
This is your memory not mine.

I explained the meaning,
pulled back your mitten,
exposed goose-pimpled flesh.

It's what they call me.

You, from Portugal
and me, India, foreign
for small towns.

In Grade Three
we had pregnant Mrs. Fields,
your parents' divorce.

Before the year was up
you disappeared, left me alone.
This is my memory not yours.

Facebook reunites us thirty years later
but it takes seven more
to meet for dinner.

We parse out memories
about olive- and brown-skinned girls,
tell each other,
     you still look the same.

Learning Lebanese

(for Reyan)

I've become a gatherer
of your words
like how other lovers
borrow clothing
dress the same.

Something well-worn,
familiar,
your mother tongue,
perhaps a forgotten dialect
from the days before
I left Zambia
my parents left India
our ancestors left Yemen.

You mimic me too
trying on sentences
that suit,
phrases foreign before
you left Liberia
your parents left Lebanon
unending cycles of leaving.

You teach me Al-Fatiha's
seven ayats,
prayers for our dead.
I explain the phrase
chosen family,
hopes for community.

Together we find
common language
for displacement
belonging
and home.

Brothers and sisters

(for Reyan)

It's been twenty-five years
since you left, and now
we drive through Beirut,
the city remains
divided
east and west
Gharbia, Sharkia.
I try to make sense of it,
map, unyielding.

You've told me it was the worst
kind of war,
        civil,
brothers and sisters
killing brothers and sisters.

Today you undertake
uneasy crossings,
veer onto streets
unfamiliar, this city
of your youth.
Here an empty house
bullet-pocked,
there Burberry boutique.

We pass a police officer,
face sun-tired
femur-long gun
dangling from shoulder
like an afterthought.

You cock an eyebrow his way:
 they used to kill us
 if we were caught
 just one block
 into the wrong side,
 had the wrong identification.

The man in fatigues turns,
his glance curious,
I swivel.

Traffic moves, we drive
already lost.
Pulling over, you lower my window,
Drakkar and dust waft in,
this darak with a bigger rifle,
pretty smile, long lashes,
maybe nineteen.
He chuckles at
your disorientation,
repeats his instructions thrice
just to be sure:
 schmel, yamin, schmel.   left, right, left.

  Yisslamo, khaye.   Thank you brother.
I close the window
exhale semiautomatic, joke:
 cops here are like
 cheerful google maps.
You shrug, inform me:
 we Lebanese like to help.

Two blocks later
old memories fill the car,
you whisper:
    I know where we are
    they used to bury us
    in open pits over there
    and over there.

I follow your finger,
faint knuckle scar, cracked nail,
pointing at the new overpass.
I squint hard,
spy ghosts hovering
under smooth cement.
One waves,
a woman in a polka-dot dress—
the kind Fairouz once wore—
I palm the window's cool glass in reply.

All the way back to the hotel,
these stories leak from you,
a relief, perhaps
as you find your Beirut.

Ageing

I know you
by your fridge
unopened jars
low-fat decisions
never tasted quite right

    I rest my fingers
    on your belly
    rolls joy
    when you laugh

I know you
by your bathroom cabinet
insecurities brush
against tooth whiteners
acne creams, attempts to
outwit ugly

    I avert my gaze, shy,
    your eyes bright stars
    in night sky

Oh! let's move
out of the city,
plant gardens,
strawberries and lilies,
grow out hair
wild and grey,
our gazes
our mirrors
and we'll believe it
when we say
you still look beautiful to me.

Sky in my veins

In last night's dream
tropical fish swam
just beneath my skin's surface,
my forearm a spy hole into
an aquarium.

They flexed and floated,
tetras, guppies, a single catfish,
sea plants swayed in the current,
a view into
an interior universe.

One winked at me
an angelfish,
veiltail waving sultry,
she taught me
to part my lips,
learn to breathe
underwater.

I awoke unafraid
for if there is an ocean
in my limbs
there must be
sky in my veins.

Attached

Crowded Istanbul airport,
you look for smoking area,
I recline on a lounge chair,
watch red light dance
under closed eyelids.

After ten minutes
a voice echoes
through terminal,
Honey? Honey?

Instant alert,
left, right, behind,
myopic,
I can't see you.

I imagine you searching,
dayaana, new word
learned this vacation:
we are lost.

I scan the terminal
attuned
to your worry
that you might not
    find me.

Find me

Get off rumbling 501 near Fifth,
look both ways,
pass laughter and smoke
puffing from corner bar.

The seniors on front stoops
wave you forward,
lifting chins
to my breeze.
Follow their directions.

Train your eye straight ahead,
catch a glimpse of me
through lilies in full bloom,
ghosts of Etobicoke's alders
who once guarded my edges.

A sliver of blue
will urge you on
one block, then two
A figment?
Keep walking.

The century-old cottages
built for me
now slump
under costly additions
waiting for slap of wet feet.

Etobicoke: an
anglicised/
colonized version
of an Anishnabe
word Wah-do-be-
kaug, meaning
"the place where
the alders grow."

Can you smell me yet?
My brine has been summoning you
from pavement and glass,
carrying whispers
of unfathomable depths.

When the asphalt ends
yes, right here,
slip off sandals
step barefoot onto sharp grass
lose your balance at my shore.

Never alone

You—who have always lived
in crowded houses
too much furniture
too many eyes
incidental contact
in every hallway
—ask me
isn't it hard to live alone?

I shake my head
but on highway bus ride
past lake and fields
to looming city,
a question:
am I living wrong?

Apartment lock clicks,
silent welcome.
I drop keys into ceramic
just to hear their clatter,
remember that C's hands
crafted the bowl.

From pockets,
used tissue, transit stub,
'free hugs' change purse,
a gift from K—
recycled bottle plastic worn smooth—
recalls tipsy singing,
waft of birthday candle smoke.

T's painting would leave behind
a rectangle of light on wallpaper
if I ever moved.
I say her name,
wonder how she is.

You gave me your old couch
and tonight, like most evenings
I settle into your indent.

My bookshelf
holds mentors
every closet,
cupboard filled
with friends.

I am never alone.

Notes and Acknowledgements

Earlier versions of "How to get wifi at Jamia Millia in 14 easy steps" and "Red Fort" were published with different titles in *Muse India* in July 2013.

Earlier versions of "Ziyarat" were published with a different title in *Siren Magazine* Toronto 2002, vol. 7.4: 15.1 and *Trikone* 2001 vol. 16.3: 11.

An earlier version of "LEIRVIK" was published a different title in *Taddle Creek*, Summer 2015.

An earlier version of "Find me," under a different title, was commissioned for the Ontario Book Publishers Organization's *What's Your Story* 2016 contest.

Earlier versions of "Some Days Are Like That" and "Rockette Lines" were published in the Sunshine Coast Festival of the Written Arts Anthology in October 2020.

"The twins of Bogotá" was inspired by "The Mixed Up Brothers of Bogotá" by Susan Dominus (*New York Times*).

"Three years in" was inspired by "Letter of Recommendation: Segmented Sleep" by Jesse Barron (*New York Times*).

"After Rumi's 'Who Makes These Changes'" is an homage to Rumi's "Who Makes These Changes."

The line *"name myself Rio and dance upon the sand"* is riffed from "Rio" (1982) by Duran Duran.

Many thanks to the Ontario Arts Council Chalmers Grant which allowed me to work with poetry mentor Sonnet L'Abbé who offered feedback on some of these poems. Our conversations about the BIPOC poetry list we read together heavily influenced how I edited this collection.

Thanks to Kathryn Payne, Manahil Bandukwala, Samantha Warwick, Vivek Shraya and Leah Horlick for reading the manuscript or specific poems and offering encouragement, advice and feedback.

Many thanks to Sharanpal Ruprai for her editorial support and to Kelsey Attard and Natalie Olsen and the rest of the Freehand team for welcoming and launching this collection.

Thanks to Rachel Letofsky, my agent at Cooke McDermid, for always having my back.

Heartfelt condolences to the family of Suzana Brito. When we reconnected, Suzy offered me the gift of shared experience and memory.

These poems were written or rewritten in my forties. Thank you to all the family and friends who loved and supported me through this decade and who were inadvertent muses for these poems.

Treats and kisses for Maggie.

And to Reyan, thank you for joining me at 43.

FARZANA DOCTOR is the Tkaronto-based author of four critically acclaimed novels: *Stealing Nasreen, Six Metres of Pavement, All Inclusive,* and *Seven. You Still Look The Same* is her debut poetry collection. Farzana is also the Maasi behind Dear Maasi, a new sex and relationships column for FGM/C survivors. She is also an activist and part-time psychotherapist.

www.linktr.ee/farzanadoctor
@farzanadoctor on Instagram and Twitter